Wild Britain

Deer

Louise and Richard Spilsbury

Heinemann
LIBRARY

www.heinemann.co.uk
Visit our website to find out more information about Heinemann Library books.

To order:
 Phone 44 (0) 1865 888066
 Send a fax to 44 (0) 1865 314091
Visit the Heinemann Bookshop at www.heinemann.co.uk to browse our catalogue and order online.

First published in Great Britain by Heinemann Library, Halley Court, Jordan Hill, Oxford OX2 8EJ, part of Harcourt Education Ltd. Heinemann is a registered trademark of Harcourt Education Ltd.

Editorial: Lucy Thunder and Helen Cannons
Design: David Poole and Celia Floyd
Illustrations: Jeff Edwards, Alan Fraser and Geoff Ward
Picture Research: Rebecca Sodergren and Peter Morris
Production: Edward Moore

Originated by Repro Multi-Warna
Printed and bound in China by South China Printing Company

The paper used to print this book comes from sustainable resources.

ISBN 0 431 03983 6
08 07 06 05 04
10 9 8 7 6 5 4 3 2 1

British Library Cataloguing in Publication Data
Spilsbury, Louise and Spilsbury, Richard
Deer. – (Wild britain)
599.6'5'0941

A full catalogue record for this book is available from the British Library.

Acknowledgements

The Publishers would like to thank the following for permission to reproduce photographs:

Ardea p12; Ardea/Ian Beames p15; Ardea/John Cancalosi p17; Ardea/M. Watson pp10, 25, 29; Ardea/S. Meyers p16; Bruce Coleman/John Cancalosi p22; Bruce Coleman/Robert Maier p4; Bruce Coleman/Hans Reinhard p23; FLPA pp14, 24; FLPA/P. Moore p27; FLPA/Silvestris p8; NHPA/Laurie Campbell pp11, 13, 21; NHPA/Manfred Danegger pp19, 20, 26; NHPA/Andy Rouse p6; NHPA/Eric Soder p28; NHPA/M. Watson p18; Oxford Scientific Films/Mark Hamblin p5; Woodfall Wild Images p9.

Cover photograph of a roe deer in its natural habitat, reproduced with permission of NHPA/Andy Rouse.

The publishers would like to thank Michael Scott for his assistance in the preparation of this book.

Every effort has been made to contact copyright holders of any material reproduced in this book. Any omissions will be rectified in subsequent printings if notice is given to the Publisher.

2617537

Contents

What are deer? 4

Where do deer live? 6

What do deer eat? 8

Finding food 10

On the move 12

Resting and sleeping 14

What is the rut? 16

Deer young 18

Growing up 20

Deer sounds 22

Under attack 24

Dangers 26

A deer's year 28

Deer in Britain 30

Glossary 31

Index 32

Any words appearing in the text in bold, **like this**, are explained in the Glossary.

What are deer?

Roe deer are quite small. They have a black stripe on their face and a white chin.

Deer are a kind of **mammal**. Deer have four legs and **hooves**. There are several kinds of deer in Britain. Roe deer are the most common. Red deer are the largest.

Red deer have red-brown coats. Male red deer have antlers and females do not.

Male deer are larger than **female** deer. Male deer are the only animals **native** to Britain that grow **antlers**. Antlers are special branched bones on a deer's head.

Where do deer live?

Woodlands provide roe deer with food and **shelter**.

Roe deer mostly live in woodland, but they may move on to farmland to feed. Red deer often live on open hills, **moors** and mountains.

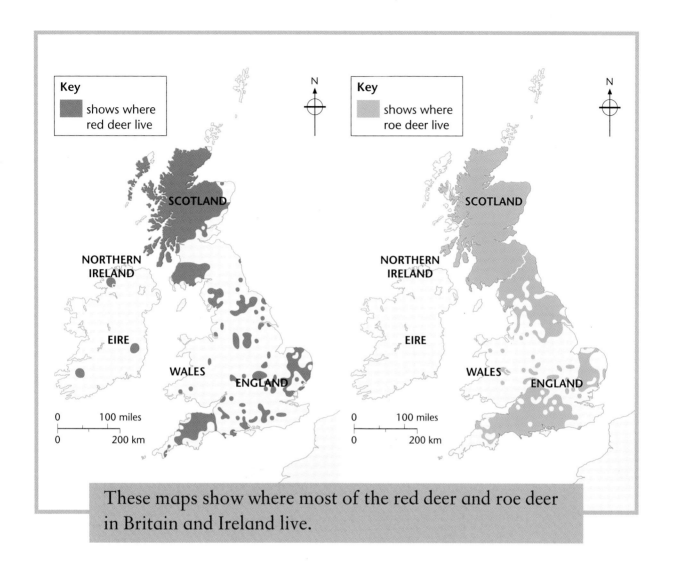

N

N

SCOTLAND

NORTHERN
IRELAND

EIRE

WALES

ENGLAND

0   100 miles

0   200 km

SCOTLAND

NORTHERN
IRELAND

EIRE

WALES

ENGLAND

0   100 miles

0   200 km

These maps show where most of the red deer and roe deer
in Britain and Ireland live.

Roe deer live in many parts of Britain.
Red deer live mainly in the Highlands
of Scotland.

What do deer eat?

Roe deer often rip off leaves from trees to eat.

Deer eat only plants. Roe deer eat **shoots**, grasses and the leaves of trees and shrubs. Red deer prefer grass, but also eat trees and shrubs.

Red deer eat heather because these plants have green leaves all through the winter.

Deer eat different plants in winter. Roe deer eat leaves from **evergreen** trees, such as holly. In winter, heather is an important food for red deer.

Finding food

Deer feed for up to ten hours each day.

Deer have a very good **sense** of smell. This helps them to find their food. Deer feed during the day, but mainly at dawn and dusk. In some areas they come out at night.

Red deer herds are usually made up only of **males**, or only of **females** and their young.

Red deer live for most of the year in large groups called **herds**. It is safer to feed in herds. Some deer can look out for danger while the others are eating.

On the move

When red deer are scared, they can leap away quickly.

Deer usually walk or trot along like horses. They can run away very quickly if something frightens them. Deer can also swim very well.

Deer often use the same routes to and from their resting places.

Deer have two **hooves** on each leg. Hooves are like long hard toes. Deer's hard hooves make paths to their favourite feeding spots.

13

Resting and sleeping

Deer rest while they chew their food for the second time.
This is called 'chewing the cud'.

Deer spend a lot of time lying down. Plant food is tough to eat so deer chew it twice. They bring food back up into their mouth from their stomach, to chew it again.

Red deer often rest in open spaces. From here they can see all around.

Deer usually sleep among leafy plants or in woods so **predators** cannot see them. If it is safe they may simply lie down where they have been feeding.

What is the rut?

Roe deer mate in summer. In this picture a male deer is sniffing a female to see if she wants to mate.

The **rut** is the time when **male** and **female** deer **mate**. Male deer chase and fight each other to win a female. Male deer fight using their **antlers** and **hooves**.

Red deer mate in autumn. Males fight by pushing against each other's antlers until one gives up and is chased away.

Male red deer try to scare other males away by showing off their big antlers. If this does not work, they fight. Male deer can be injured or even killed in these battles.

Deer young

Baby deer have a spotted coat and no smell. This helps to hide them from **predators**.

Most baby roe and red deer are born between May and June. At first they cannot walk far. Their mother hides them in long grass when she goes off to feed.

These young roe deer, like all deer, suckle standing up.

Like all baby **mammals,** young deer feed by drinking milk from their mother's body. This is called **suckling**.

Growing up

This young roe deer is going with its mother to find good plants or grass to eat.

After a month or two young deer follow their mother when she goes to find food. They begin to eat plants. They still **suckle** for several months, too.

Young **males** begin to grow **antlers** between eight and twelve months of age. This is a young roe deer.

At two months old the spots on a baby deer's coat fade. Young roe deer stay with their mother for up to fourteen months. Then they leave to have young of their own.

Deer sounds

Male red deer try to chase off other males during the rut by roaring. This saves them having to fight.

Deer make sounds to tell each other things. Roe deer make a barking sound like a dog to warn other deer of danger. **Male** red deer roar during the **rut** to scare other males.

Young deer squeak or bleat to keep in touch with their mothers.

Sounds are useful in places like woods where deer cannot see each other. Mother deer call their young to them. Young deer scream if something frightens or attacks them.

Under attack

Foxes may attack weak or old adult roe deer, as well as young ones.

Foxes and badgers sometimes catch young deer to eat. Some large birds, such as golden eagles, also hunt baby deer. Only about one in every ten deer reach their first birthday.

Roe deer have a short stubby tail with a white patch around it. The patch shows when they run from danger.

Deer watch and listen for danger. They can also smell some **predators**. When roe deer run away their white tail patch warns other deer that danger is near.

Dangers

Every year between 30,000 to 50,000 road accidents in Britain involve deer.

Roe deer usually live for eight to ten years. Red deer can live for up to 25 years. One of the greatest dangers for deer is traffic. Many are injured when they cross roads.

Many people dislike hunting, but hunters say they help look after **herds** of red deer in Scotland.

In parts of Scotland red deer are fed and encouraged on to land by **hunters**. Some deer are shot, but hunting is the reason the land is kept safe for other deer.

A deer's year

This female roe deer is moulting. Her coat will change from a brown-grey winter coat to chestnut-red.

Roe and red deer **moult** in spring. Their hair falls out so they can grow a healthy new coat. Red deer grow a new red coat for summer. It turns brown or grey by winter.

This male red deer's new antlers are growing. The antlers are covered in furry grey skin called 'velvet'.

Once a year a **male** deer's **antlers** fall off and it grows new ones. Red deer lose and regrow their antlers in spring and summer. Roe deer replace their antlers in winter.

Deer in Britain

As well as roe deer and red deer, there are four other kinds of wild deer that live in Britain. What differences can you see between these three below and the roe and red deer?

muntjac

fallow deer

sika

The artwork on this page is not to scale.

Glossary

antlers special bones that grow on a male deer's head

evergreen tree or plant that keeps most of its leaves all year round

female animal that can become a mother when it is grown up

herds groups of large plant-eating animals

hooves long hard toes

hunters people who chase and kill animals

male animal that can become a father when it is grown up

mammals group of animals that feed their babies their own milk and have some hair on their bodies.

mate when a male and female come together to make babies

moors cool windy area, usually quite high up a hill

moult when an animal loses its old coat of hair

native type of animal that has lived in a country for a long time

predator animal that catches and eats other animals for food

rut time of year when male deer fight to win a female to mate with

senses most animals have five senses – sight, hearing, touch, taste and smell

shelter somewhere safe to stay, live and have young

shoots young stem, leaves and flowers of a plant

suckle/suckling when a mother feeds her baby with milk from her body

Index

antlers   5, 16, 21, 29

baby deer   18, 19, 20

females   5, 16, 18, 19, 20, 21, 23

fighting (rut)   16, 17, 22

food   8, 9, 14

herds (deer group)   16, 17, 22

hooves   4, 13, 16

hunting   27

males   5, 16, 17, 22

moulting   28

red deer   6, 9, 11, 12, 15, 17, 18, 22, 28, 29

roe deer   6, 8, 18, 20, 21, 24, 25, 28, 29

smelling   10, 25

suckling   19, 20

winter   9, 29

Titles in the *Wild Britain* series include:

Hardback   0 431 03981 X

Hardback   0 431 03985 2

Hardback   0 431 03983 6

Hardback   0 431 03930 5

Hardback   0 431 03984 4

Hardback   0 431 03931 3

Hardback   0 431 03982 8

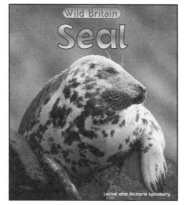

Hardback   0 431 03933 X

Hardback   0 431 03929 1

Find out about the other titles in this series on our website www.heinemann.co.uk/library